There's a Wolf 🐾 in the Classroom!

There's a Wolf in the Classroom!

Bruce Weide & Patricia Tucker

Carolrhoda Books, Inc./Minneapolis

Pat, Bruce, Koani, and Indy would like to thank ABC/Kane and Dutcher Productions, the Fanwood Foundation, Half Price Books, National Wildlife Federation, Patagonia, Sharpe Communications, the Wolf Education & Research Center, the Montana Natural History Center, and individuals too numerous to list for supporting and believing in Wild Sentry; you made this story possible.

We greatly appreciate Dorothy Hinshaw Patent's encouragement and help as well as the editorial work of Amy Gelman. Thank you Graham Neale for wolf-sitting.

This book is available in two editions:
Library binding by Carolrhoda Books, Inc.
Soft cover by First Avenue Editions

Carolrhoda Books, Inc., and First Avenue Editions
c/o The Lerner Group
241 First Avenue North, Minneapolis, MN 55401

LIBRARY OF CONGRESS CATALOGING-IN-PUBLICATION INFORMATION

Weide, Bruce.

    There's a wolf in the classroom! / by Bruce Weide and
Patricia Tucker.
        p. cm.
    Includes index.
    ISBN 0-87614-939-5 (lib. bdg.)
    ISBN 0-87614-958-1 (pbk.)
    1. Wolves as pets—Juvenile literature. 2. Wolves—Juvenile literature. [1. Wolves as pets. 2. Wolves.] I. Tucker, Patricia A. II. Title.
SF459.W63W45 1995   94-42673
                                                              CIP
                                                              AC

Manufactured in the United States of America

1 2 3 4 5 6 – JR – 00 99 98 97 96 95

Dedicated to Koani—may her work as an ambassador wolf inspire people to preserve wild places where her kin can run free.

"In wilderness is the preservation of the world."
—Henry David Thoreau 1817–1862

Contents

Introduction
The Gray Wolf: A Natural History

Contrary to what's been said about them in folklore, fairy tales, stories and movies, wolves are not dangerous to people. Even when wildlife biologists come near their food or pups, wolves back away and act shy and unaggressive.

The movie and book *Never Cry Wolf* showed wolves making a living by eating mice. While wolves do eat mice and small rodents, they're like an after-school snack is to you —appetizing but not enough to live on. Wolves mostly eat large animals such as deer, elk, caribou, musk ox, bison, and moose.

Wolves weigh 60 to 130 pounds. A moose can easily weigh 1,000 pounds. Teeth are the only thing that a wolf has to bring down a large animal like a moose. Imagine yourself walking up to an animal as big as a horse and trying to take a bite out of him. Is he going to sit there and let you make lunch out of him? No way! He's going to kick and stomp. It's not uncommon for a wolf to be hurt or killed while hunting. This is why wolves try to find the old, sick, weak, and young prey animals, which won't be as dangerous as healthy animals.

This is also why wolves hunt in a group—there's strength in numbers. A group of wolves is called a pack. A pack is a family of wolves, not just a group of wolves that said, "Hey, it's Friday night, let's go out for a hunt." There are 4 to 15 wolves in a pack. Pack size depends on what the wolves prey on. A large animal such as an elk or moose is more difficult and dangerous to bring down than a smaller animal such as a deer. The more wolves there are in a pack, the larger the animals a pack can hunt. If wolves hunt deer, they tend to live in a smaller pack. Wolves that hunt elk or moose need to live in larger packs. A pack of wolves lives in a territory that's 50 to 2,000 square miles in size. The size of a territory depends on the number of prey animals that live there.

Wolves communicate in a number of ways that include facial expressions and the way they hold their tails and ears. They also leave messages by scent-marking on stumps and shrubs with urine. The form of communication that wolves are famous for is howling. Wolves howl to locate members of their pack, to warn strange wolves to stay out of their territory, and as a ceremony that helps the wolves feel closer to each other. Who knows, maybe wolves howl for fun, too.

Sometimes wolves kill livestock. In Alberta and British Columbia, Canada, where thousands of wolves live near cattle, they kill less than one cow out of a thousand. While that isn't very many cows, people who want wolves brought back to the places where they once lived need to understand the concerns of individual ranchers who lose cattle—the animals that provide their living—to wolves. On the other hand, people who don't like wolves need to understand that a majority of Americans (two-thirds) want wolves to be brought back. We live in a democracy. Both sides need to listen to and respect each other's opinions and work toward solutions. Shouting at each other never solves anything; it only causes more problems and misunderstandings.

Chapter 1
In the Beginning

The tiny black wolf squirmed in Pat's arms. A whimper came from the bundle of soft fur. The two-week old pup nuzzled blindly for the nipple of the bottle. She found it and sucked greedily as milk dribbled down her chin. Pat watched the pup's belly swell with warm milk and noticed a pair of eyes staring up at her. Pat exclaimed, "Look, her eyes just opened!" Like many young mammals, the pup's eyes were blue. Later the eyes would change to the piercing yellow that wolves are famous for.

Pat bottle-feeds Koani, moments before the wolf pup opened her eyes for the first time.

Even as a pup, Koani wasn't camera-shy.

The first thing the pup ever saw was Pat. The second thing she saw was Bruce. After the pup finished feeding, Bruce rubbed her fat belly with a warm, wet washcloth. This helped the pup to urinate and defecate, or pee and poop. In the wild, the wolf mother's warm, wet tongue would do this.

Bruce set the pup down in the playpen, where she promptly fell asleep snuggled in with her brothers and sister. Like most wolves in the United States (outside of Alaska), these pups were born in captivity, in a protected area. The five pups were going to be part of a television documentary about wolves.

9

Pat holds Koani and her brother, aged four weeks.

Wolves **bond,** or form close relationships, with their pack members at a very young age. They are cautious and suspicious of strange things. Wolves that live in captivity, where people will be part of their lives, need to bond with people or they will be scared and unhappy. Because of this, the pups had been separated from their mother at the age of two weeks old. That way they would grow up to feel comfortable around humans. In the wild, pups are constantly with their mother for the first four weeks of their lives. After that, the entire pack helps to raise the pups. Wild pups wouldn't be alone until they are at least six months old.

For the next couple weeks, the young pups needed to be fed every four hours. The alarm clock buzzed in the middle of the night. Pat and Bruce woke up. With eyes nearly closed from sleepiness, they warmed milk on the stove, filled bottles, and stumbled to the playpen full of hungry pups.

One day the television filmmaker said, "Pat, you're a wildlife biologist and Bruce is a storyteller. You both know how to teach children about wolves. Would you raise one of the pups so that I can film you taking it to classrooms?"

"That would be a big responsibility," said Pat. "We need to think about it." Bruce and Pat talked about the job of living with a wolf. After all, it could live to the age of 15. All of its life, the wolf would be like a curious and unruly, 2-year-old human child with sharp teeth and powerful jaws.

Bruce and Pat also realized that raising a wolf could be dangerous, not because wolves are vicious but because some people are. Politicians, ranchers, environmentalists, hunters and others had been arguing over whether or not wolves should be returned to Yellowstone, the world's first national park. Wolves used to live in Yellowstone National Park until they were **exterminated**—hunted until no more were left alive—about 50 years ago. In fact, wolves once ranged throughout most of North America. But when Europeans first sailed across the Atlantic Ocean to settle in a new land that would become the United States, they brought their fear and hatred of wolves with them. Everywhere they went, they trapped, poisoned, and shot wolves. In the late 1800s, ranchers hired men called **wolfers** to do one job—kill all the wolves they could. By the 1930s, all the wolves in the lower 48 states (the United States except for Alaska and Hawaii) were dead except for some that lived in a large wilderness area in northern Minnesota. Half a century later, attitudes toward the wolf began to change. Some people realized that the big, bad wolf existed only in stories. Wildlife biologists studied wolves, and people learned that wolves

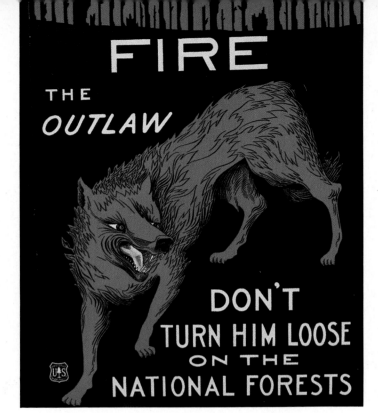

This Forest Service poster from 1942 shows the attitude some people have toward wolves.

weren't evil animals. Many Americans wanted wolves returned to Yellowstone—brought back there and allowed to live freely. However, Pat and Bruce knew that many people still hated wolves because they misunderstood them. Some people believed that wolves killed lots of cows and sheep. Other people still believed that wolves ate humans. Most people who hated wolves had never seen one except in their imaginations.

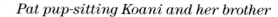
Pat pup-sitting Koani and her brother

"Some people hate wolves so much, they might try to kill the wolf we're raising," said Pat. "We'd have to be very protective."

"Some of those people are mad enough about wolves to want to kill us," added Bruce. "But if wolves are ever going to run wild and free in the northern Rockies again, people need to learn what they're really like."

Finally, Pat and Bruce made a decision. "We'll do it," they told the filmmaker.

"Which pup do you think would be best?" he responded.

Pat looked down at the three black and two gray pups that wrestled and played on the floor. She pointed at the pup pulling on her brother's tail. "Let's take that playful black pup. A lot of people think black wolves are different from gray or white wolves. We can help people understand that color doesn't make any difference in wolves, just like with humans."

"What shall we name her?" asked Bruce The three of them sat there and thought about names.

"Koani," said the filmmaker. "That means 'play' in the language of Blackfeet Native Americans."

"She is playful," said Pat.

"When she grows up, Koani will be a teacher," the filmmaker said. "The three of you can help students learn that wolves aren't big and bad."

13

Koani at three months, at her new home

Chapter 2
Indy: A Legend in His Own Mind

A few weeks later, Koani arrived at her new home in Montana. Bruce and Pat had worked hard to prepare a secure place for Koani to live. A 10-foot-tall fence surrounded an area almost the size of a football field. Aspens and pine trees provided shade. A stream flowed through it. A shelter filled with sweet straw gave her a place to sleep during rainy days. An elevated platform allowed her to look out over her surroundings. Koani explored her pen with Pat and Bruce. She romped and played in the tall grass and cool stream. But something was missing.

The minute Bruce and Pat left the pen and walked into the house, Koani made it known that she was lonely. She started with a whimper and progressed to a whine that rose to full-pitched frantic howls. Koani needed a friend who could be with her all the time. Koani was not spoiled. In the wild, a wolf pup never spends a moment alone, without other pack members, for the first six months of its life. Wolves are very social animals. Bruce and Pat knew that leaving Koani alone was cruel.

So they took turns staying with Koani. One of them always remained in the pen watching, petting, playing or sleeping with her. They knew they couldn't do this forever. Koani needed a friend who didn't have to leave the pen to answer the phone or cook meals or go to the bathroom. Koani needed a **canine** companion. A dog, a member of the same animal family as wolves, would be the perfect playmate for Koani.

In the animal shelter, Pat looked at all the dogs. One dog, number 27, bounced up and down like popcorn. Every time his head appeared, Pat saw a happy grin.

At home, she told Bruce about the popcorn dog. "We'll go to the animal shelter and see him tomorrow," said Pat.

"Maybe you'd better call the animal shelter and tell them we want to see number 27 in the morning," said Bruce.

Pat looked at her watch. "I'd better hurry. The animal shelter closes in five minutes."

"It's a good thing you called," said the woman at the animal shelter. "We have too many dogs and more just came in. It's sad but we have to **euthanize** some. Number 27 is at the top of the list."

"Thank goodness I called," said Pat. "We'll be there to pick him up first thing in the morning."

Early the next day, Bruce and Pat found a friend to puppy-sit Koani and drove to the animal shelter. As they returned home, number 27 stood between them, wagging his tail and licking their faces. "He needs a name," said Pat as she stroked his head.

"Let's name him after the adventure-movie character Indiana Jones," said Bruce. "After all, he'll have a wolf for a companion, and he escaped death with only moments to spare. We'll call him Indy for short." Indy licked their faces. He seemed proud of his new name.

Indy, originally known as dog number 27 at the animal shelter

Koani and Indy get to know each other by playing together.

When Koani saw Indy, she went wild with excitement. Her ears lay flat on her head. She tucked her tail between her legs and licked all over Indy's face. Then she flopped onto her back, whimpering and pawing. With this behavior, she displayed her respect for an older, wiser canine. As you'll see later, Koani's way of meeting strange dogs changed dramat-ically later on, when she became an adult.

Indy, who was six months older than Koani, tolerated her puppy silliness. He growled softly and sniffed Koani thoroughly, all the time holding his tail high. With this behavior, Indy showed that he was **dominant.** Koani thought he was wonderful.

A recording of wolf howls catches Koani's attention.

Chapter 3
Take a Walk on the Wild Side

Human civilization is wild to a wolf. Sidewalks scared Koani. Bikes frightened her. Cars terrified her. People and dogs are used to seeing planes, fire engines, and trains pass by. To an animal like a wolf, these things are strange and dangerous. Many weeks passed before Bruce and Pat could cross a road without having to drag Koani. In Koani's eyes, people who wore backpacks or bicycle helmets were monsters. If she saw such a person, she jerked frantically at the leash and quivered with fear.

Walking a wolf is not at all like walking a dog. Anything that didn't scare Koani needed to be explored. Wolves investigate things with their noses and teeth. On her sixty-foot leash, she dashed about and managed to grab things that interested her. Koani snatched newspapers from porches and shredded them. She pulled trash out of cans and ripped it to pieces. She even enjoyed crushing aluminum cans she discovered in bushes. Once, she found an unopened can of soda pop. She rolled the can along the ground while biting at it. Finally, her needle-sharp baby teeth punctured the can. With a loud hiss, the can spun like a top and sprayed soda pop on Koani. She jumped back in alarm and then pounced on it with delight, snapping at the spurting sweet liquid.

In the wild, wolves are most active during dawn and dusk, for about four hours a day. The rest of the time, wolves nap or hang out. Koani was no different. So, every day, morning and evening, at dawn and dusk, Pat and Bruce walked Koani and Indy. Each walk lasted two hours. No matter what, come rain or snow, on Christmas Day or during Saturday morning cartoons, Bruce and Pat walked Koani. Without her walks, Koani would have been bored and paced back and forth in her pen or tried to escape.

Koani enjoys one of her favorite puppy pastimes—ripping apart a box.

Left: *Koani must have thought this sign was referring to her.* Above: *Koani and Pat play chase.*

From the age of four to seven months, it became more and more difficult to walk Koani. She grew at the rate of half a pound each day. Wolves in the wild grow this fast also and the pup's mother, father, aunts and uncles have to work hard to feed them. As Koani grew, her strength increased. During

a walk through a very wet meadow, Bruce watched as Koani tried to find deer mice in the tall grass. Without knowing it, Bruce stepped into a loop of Koani's loose leash. Suddenly, Koani bolted and ran as fast as she could. She had spotted some strange dogs and wanted to chase them out of her territory. The leash tightened, the loop closed around Bruce's legs, and jerked them out from beneath him. Koani was so strong and ran so fast that she dragged Bruce across the soggy meadow feetfirst and on his back. Water splashed all around him. He looked like a water-skier who had fallen but wouldn't let go of the ski rope.

Koani investigates the teeter-totter in her pen.

Pat and Bruce knew that Koani needed more than the two walks a day to keep her occupied and happy. They built toys and put them in Koani's pen. She loved the teeter-totter. By placing her front feet on one end and her back feet on the other, Koani learned how to rock it back and forth all by herself. In another favorite game, Bruce or Pat covered Koani with a blanket and played peekaboo. Koani also delighted in ripping up cardboard boxes, plastic milk jugs, ice cream cartons, and discarded stuffed toys. Every day, the four of them bounced on their Montana Trampoline, which they created by placing a piece of plywood on top of four stacks of old tires.

At the end of a day, Bruce and Pat fell into bed exhausted. "When we take Koani on her two walks, she's totally out of control," said Pat. "How can we ever hope to take her into a classroom?"

"We have to," said Bruce. "Koani is a teacher. She's not a pet. This is a very strange life we've introduced her to. Wolves are used to trees, rivers, mountains, and meadows, not people, streets, buildings, and cars. We'll just have to keep working to get her used to living this way."

Pat, Koani, and Indy on a wolf walk

Chapter 4
What's a Nice Little Wolf Like You Doing in a Place Like This?

A group of wolves that live together is called a pack. A group of people who live together is called a family. Bruce and Pat's family consisted of themselves, a wolf and a dog. Koani's pack consisted of herself, a dog and two humans. You could say that Bruce and Pat had an odd family and Koani lived in a peculiar pack.

In a wolf pack, there is an **alpha** male and female. The alpha wolves are the leaders or, as wildlife biologists call them, the dominant animals. Even though Koani knew that Pat and Bruce weren't wolves, she saw them as the alpha animals in her pack. Indy was like an older brother to Koani. Even after she grew to twice Indy's size, Koani would roll on her back and **submit** to him. Indy understood his power as an older brother. Sometimes he gathered all the bones in a pile. If Koani tried to take a bone, Indy growled and snapped at her. He drove her away.

Even though Koani's teeth are bared, she and Indy are just playing. Notice how small Koani's teeth are. Those are baby teeth that later fell out and were replaced by larger adult teeth.

Being the oldest didn't make Indy the smartest. Koani quickly learned he was easily distracted and could be tricked. For example, she would walk away from Indy and the pile of bones and pretend to find something of great interest in the grass. Indy would rush over to see what she had found. Koani would then dash to the bone pile and grab one. This often resulted in a noisy fight. Indy would growl and snarl ferociously while Koani squealed, snapped, and whined. No one ever got hurt badly. Just like fights between human sisters and brothers, these squabbles were mostly noise. Neither wanted to injure the other. The same is true of wild wolves, most of the time.

In addition to the members of her pack, Koani had three important friends—Chloe Dog Cook, the Great Dane; Elliot Steele, the German Shepherd; and Gray Neale, a human. Koani met Chloe Dog Cook while out on walks. They became instant friends. At first, Chloe Dog Cook didn't know how to play. Koani and Indy taught her to wrestle, chase, and play tag. Even after Koani grew to full-size, Chloe Dog Cook was big enough to wrestle her to the ground and pin her. Chloe Dog Cook enjoyed her time with Koani and Indy so much that she sat beside the window for hours, waiting for them to walk by.

Elliot Steele was the same age as Koani and also lived nearby. He was a clumsy dog with wobbly legs who lived for one thing—to play. Koani fell in love with him instantly. She flirted and played hard-to-get. Their favorite game was chase. With Koani's ability to make sharp turns and run fast, Elliot Steele never caught her. But to keep him interested, she'd almost let him. Then she shifted into high gear and sped away again.

Koani with her friends Chloe Dog Cook (left) and Elliot Steele (right).

24

Gray Neale wrestles with Koani. Koani has to be the one to start a wrestling match; you can't roughhouse with her at any time the way you can with a dog.

Indy frowned on the fun Elliot Steele and Koani shared. Indy beat up on Elliot. Elliot Steele thought Indy was playing and considered him a good buddy.

Besides Bruce and Pat, Gray was the only other person who could take Koani on walks. Koani adored Uncle Gray. He invented toys for her to play with like the bones he hung from a tree limb on a bungee cord. He made piñatas full of dog treats. Because he didn't have to go out on wolf walks every day like Bruce and Pat, Gray allowed Koani to lead him through swamps, brambles, and thickets.

Pat and Bruce tended to get grumpy about such side-trips.

Koani had a good memory. Even after she grew up, she remembered people and dogs that she'd met in her puppyhood. She greeted them with enthusiastic muzzle-nuzzles, just like the face-licks pack members greet each other with in the wild. Indy also licked faces. Face-licking is a wolf behavior that remains in most dogs. Even though some people don't like dogs to lick them, the dog is only trying to act polite.

Muzzle-licking begins when wolf puppies are four to five weeks old. After a successful hunt, the adult wolves return to the den. Their bellies are swollen with fresh meat, as much as 20 pounds. You'd have to eat 60 to 70 hamburgers or way more than 100 jumbo hot dogs to put that much meat in your stomach. The puppies rush out to greet the adults, jump up and lick their faces. This causes the adult to throw up, or **regurgitate,** and the pups have a nice hot meal. As the pups mature, face-licking becomes the proper way to greet dominant pack members. Face-licking is a wolf's way of shaking hands; it's polite canine manners.

Once, on a walk, after she had just eaten, Koani met two dog puppies that were younger than she was. They licked around her face. Much to their delight, Koani regurgitated. The pups happily ate the half-digested meat, their tails wagging enthusiastically. Koani watched with a pleased look on her face. Pat and Bruce didn't feel so happy. The pups were eating five dollars worth of meat meant to nourish Koani.

Koani gives Pat (top) and Chloe Dog Cook (bottom) muzzle licks as greetings. Much like the human handshake, this behavior shows friendliness.

Koani demonstrates some of the reasons she can't be a pet. After shredding the pillowcase in the picture at left, she wanted to play peekaboo with it.

Chapter 5
Koani is a Good Wolf, But She's a Bad Dog

Even though Koani was friendly with dogs and people that she knew, she showed early on that she wasn't a good pet. The first time Bruce and Pat let Koani in the house, she leaped onto the counter, broke two dinner plates, and spilled a pitcher of milk. From the counter, she sprang to the table, scattering silverware, cups, and food. The table tipped over and scared her silly. She dove onto the couch. For 15 seconds, she lay there looking as pleased and contented as a big, lazy dog. Then her yellow eyes focused on the upholstery buttons attached to the backrest of the couch. Pop, pop, pop! With lightning speed, Koani ripped the buttons off.

Pat pulled her off the couch, but not before Koani managed to shred a pillow and shake it about. As pillow feathers floated down, Pat said, "She may be a good wolf, but she's a bad dog. Anybody who thinks that wolves make good pets is crazy."

"Let's hope she becomes a good teacher," said Bruce. "After all, that's why we have her."

Sometimes Pat and Bruce brought Indy into the house. But Koani hated to be left alone. Just as she had when she was a puppy, she howled. One of the reasons that wolves howl is to locate other pack members. If you were on a hike and got separated from the group, you'd shout or whistle to locate the others.

"It doesn't seem fair to never have Indy in the house," said Pat.

"It's not fair to leave Koani alone in the pen either," said Bruce. "But unless we want our furniture destroyed, she can't be in the house. Wolves don't obey commands like dogs."

"Plus she can't be housebroken," said Pat. It's not that wolves are dumb. Koani urinated in the house to show that the place was hers or, as wildlife biologists say, to mark her territory. Wolves are very **territorial.** That's another reason they howl, to warn strange wolves to stay out of their territory. Property is what humans call their territory. If strangers walked through your backyard, you might shout at them to leave.

"I've got an idea!" said Pat. "We could fence off part of the living room and build a dog door so that she can come from her outside pen into an inside pen."

So that's what Bruce and Pat did. They even dug a tunnel 40 feet long that connected Koani's enclosure with their earth-sheltered house. At first Koani viewed the swinging dog door with suspicion. After three weeks, she realized it wasn't a trap. Koani enjoyed being able to check up on her pack members whenever she wanted. Like humans, wolves are naturally social; it's in their nature, they can't help it.

Above: *Koani cautiously comes through the tunnel from her outdoor enclosure to her indoor pen.*
Right: *Koani in her indoor enclosure with Bruce.*

However, in captivity the predatory instinct is another reason why wolves are not good pets. A captive wolf learns not to fear people, but it will never lose its instincts. A child running and shouting causes the same predatory reaction in a captive wolf as would a prey animal. The wolf isn't being mean, it's just the way he or she was made. Because of Koani's predatory instincts, Pat and Bruce never let her off the leash during walks. It's important to remember, however, that wild wolves are very shy and afraid of people. There has never been a recorded case of a healthy, wild wolf killing anyone in North America.

Left: *Koani chews on an elk.* Below: *Koani's raised tail and the fur standing up on her back serve as a warning to a strange dog not to enter her territory.*

Wolves are **predators;** therefore, they possess predatory **instincts.** A predator is an animal that survives by eating other animals. When a predator like a wolf sees an animal run, they instinctively chase and try to kill it. If wild wolves didn't have this instinct, they'd starve to death. After all, there aren't any fast-food restaurants or grocery stores in the wild.

Koani has bonded to Bruce and Pat, but she still has predatory instincts. Here, guarding her food, she snarls at Bruce as he approaches to take her picture.

As Koani grew older, she became less submissive and more aggressive to strange dogs. This change in behavior came from the instinct of adult wolves to guard territory. Wild wolves chase wolves that aren't members of the pack out of their territory; sometimes they even kill trespassers. Another instinct of wolves is that possession is 100 percent of the law. Bruce and Pat learned that if they tried to take anything away from Koani, she would bite. Because of this, they worked to make sure that she didn't get hold of anything valuable. But that didn't always work.

One night, just after Halloween, Bruce went out to check on Koani. He petted her and she lay in the straw with her eyes closed, or so it appeared. He set the flashlight down. Suddenly, Koani snatched the flashlight and dashed away. As she ran in the darkness with the light shining inside her mouth, she looked like a wolf-o'-lantern or something from a scary story. Eventually, she lay down and chewed on the flashlight. Bruce slowly reached for the flashlight. Koani growled. Bruce's fingers touched the light. Faster than a bolt of lightning, Koani's jaws clamped on his wrist. Obviously Koani didn't bite as hard as she could or she'd have snapped his hand off. Nevertheless, the bite left a big purple bruise. Bruce rolled Koani on her back and held her down by the ruff while glaring into her eyes. He growled at her. This is how an alpha wolf dominates a pack member and also the way that dogs dominate each other. After a tense moment Koani relaxed and looked away. The fight was over. Bruce released her. She stood up, whined softly and licked his face. He petted and reassured her.

With her ears laid back, Koani is telling Elliot Steele that she wants to be friendly. Wolves and dogs have many similarities, including the ways they communicate, but there are important differences between them.

In some ways, Koani and Indy behaved alike. For example, like Koani, Indy licked faces to show submission and to beg for attention. He chased rabbits and squirrels, marked territory by urinating, buried bones, and became upset when strange canines entered his territory. Nevertheless, they also acted quite different. Dogs' ancestors are wolves, but for fifteen thousand years dogs have been specially bred to live with people. Dogs that disobeyed or bit people were killed. People only allowed dogs who obeyed commands to have puppies. Eventually, dogs lost many of the instincts that make a wolf a bad companion for humans. Breeding animals to behave and look the way that we want them to is called **domestication.** Indy was domesticated. You could call him—and any dog—a domesticated wolf. Though Koani behaved in a tame manner around people, she was wild at heart and couldn't be expected to act like a dog. One look into Koani's piercing yellow eyes could convince you she wasn't domesticated.

Bruce and Pat thought about how much their lives had changed since Koani entered the picture. They'd had an expensive pen built on an acre of their land and fenced off part of the living room for a wolf. They couldn't go away together; after all, there weren't any wolf-sitters in the phone book. They'd both given up jobs to devote their time to preparing Koani for classroom visits. They hoped it would work.

Chapter 6
How Does a Wolf Get Ready for School?

If Koani was going to visit schools, the first thing she had to get used to was traveling inside her kennel in the van. No matter how much time Pat or Bruce spent trying, Koani refused to enter the van without a struggle. Sometimes she even bit them to express her frustration. Indy, on the other hand, leaped into the van as soon as the door opened. He wanted to make sure to get his place on the bus. Koani never overcame her dislike of vehicles. She demonstrated in every way possible that if travel was necessary, she'd just as soon walk.

Koani lets Bruce know that she doesn't want to get into the van.

Accompanied by Pat and Indy, Koani enters a school for the first time.

To people, there's nothing unusual about doors. But to Koani, doors looked dangerous. It took two weeks for Koani to realize a door wasn't a trap. The next step was taking her inside a building. During the summer, when the students weren't there, Bruce and Pat got permission to enter the elementary school down the road from them.

Pat opened the school door. Indy dashed inside. Koani sniffed the entry way and followed cautiously. The hard, polished floor felt strange and slippery to her feet. With her tail tucked between her legs, she stood still and suspiciously eyed the hallway. Pat slowly closed the door. Filled with panic, Koani whirled around and scratched at the door. Bruce petted and reassured her. Then she saw Indy at the end of the hall, his nose in a trash can. Her ears pricked up. Koani walked toward Indy with her legs spread apart so that she wouldn't slip.

34

Left: *Pat and Koani explore a school stage.* Below: *Koani practices getting used to things that are ordinarily unfamiliar to wolves.*

For the next few weeks, they explored the school. They ran up and down stairs, knocked over trash cans, chased basketballs in the gymnasium, and even tried out the fire escape. The fire escape stairs were made of metal gratings, which meant that you could see through them down to the ground. Surprisingly, this scared Indy but not Koani.

The first time Koani investigated a drinking fountain, she jumped back in alarm when

Bruce turned on the water. In a classroom, Koani licked the chalkboard. Then she noticed an eraser. She grabbed it and dashed away, running through the aisles between rows of desks with Indy in hot pursuit. Finally, the game ended after Koani tore the eraser to shreds. Pat and Bruce left a note and money for a new eraser, hoping that the teacher would understand when she returned to her classroom in the fall.

Koani stalked back and forth through the aisles of seats in the auditorium. To her delight, she discovered a treasure stuck to the bottom of a chair. With her front teeth, she carefully plucked the wad of pink gum and chewed it in preparation to swallow. But no matter how much she chewed, the gum never broke apart. Finally she spit it out and looked for a fresh piece. Forever after, whenever Koani first entered an auditorium, she searched chair bottoms for gum.

With each new adventure, Bruce and Pat noticed something. Koani waited for Indy to take the lead. When he showed no fear, she followed. Indy was more than a good friend to Koani. As a dog, he didn't fear new things the way a wolf would. This meant that Indy could lead Koani into places where she wouldn't have ventured without him.

Koani explores a lecture hall by looking for gum under the desks.

Another step in preparing Koani to be a teacher was making her feel comfortable around strangers. On walks, if people showed interest, Bruce and Pat asked them to kneel and let Koani approach. Eventually, Koani sniffed the people and licked their faces. Even after she became an adult, Koani greeted new people in this friendly manner.

Once, as Koani licked a woman's cheek, the woman said, "It looks a lot like a wolf."

"She is," said Bruce.

The woman froze in fear. "Wolves are dangerous, aren't they?"

"You're not in any danger," said Bruce. "By licking your face, Koani is telling you that she isn't a threat. Besides, you put yourself in more danger driving to the store than you would by walking through a forest full of wolves."

As they talked, the woman slowly relaxed. By the time the woman stood up to leave, she had a new attitude about wolves. Koani had taught her first lesson as a teacher.

After hundreds of hours working with Koani, Bruce and Pat decided they'd done all that they could to prepare her for the first school program. A big question remained. How would Koani react to being inside a classroom full of strangers?

In preparation for a school visit, Pat allows Koani to meet two young girls to help her get used to being around students.

Koani gets used to the wolf van.

Chapter 7
The Big Day: Koani Goes to School (And Of Course, So Does Indy)

In a small Montana town, Bruce parked the van in front of the school. Beside him, Pat stared out the windshield but didn't speak. To the west, snow covered mountains rose behind tall pine trees. Cattle gazed behind barbed-wire fences. Inside the van, Koani paced nervously. Indy lay peacefully on his pad atop a storage box. Finally, Bruce and Pat looked at each other. "How do you think Koani will act?" said Pat. "Do you think she'll panic once we get inside with all the students?"

"We'll never know until we do it," said Bruce. They climbed out of the van and walked to the classroom.

Left: *Getting ready to go to class.* Above: *Pat shows how to howl like a wolf.*

Thirty-two fourth-graders enthusiastically greeted Bruce and Pat. "Where's the wolf?" a student called out. "Are we really going to see a real wolf?" asked another. "Will the wolf bite us?"

The teacher quieted the students, and the program began. Pat, the wildlife biologist, explained to the class how wolves live together, what they eat, how pups are raised, and what they need to survive. Bruce, the writer and storyteller, told the story of Little Red Riding Hood. Then he said, "All stories, even the make-believe tales, contain lessons. What's the real lesson in Little Red Riding Hood? You're all smart enough to know that it isn't a story about avoiding wolves that dress up in nightgowns. This is a story about obedience, self-discipline and doing what your parents tell you to do. Little Red Riding Hood did two things her mother told her not to do. She stepped off the straight and narrow trail to pick flowers for Grandma and spoke to a stranger. The wolf in the story plays the role of a stranger—just like actors play roles in movies. The wolf also plays the role of villain in other stories such as 'The Three Little Pigs,' 'Peter and the Wolf,' or movies such as *Beauty and the Beast.*"

Finally, the time arrived to introduce Koani. "Remember to keep her on a tight leash," whispered Pat. "And be prepared for students trying to reach out and touch her."

While Bruce headed for the van to get Koani, Pat spoke to the class, "Think of how you'd feel if you walked into a strange place filled with wolves." A nervous laugh came from the students. "How would you want them to act?" Pat asked.

A girl said, "I'd want them to be quiet and sit still."

"That's exactly how Koani will want you to act," said Pat.

Another student blurted out, "Can we pet her?"

"I'm sorry, but you can't. I know that would be fun, but you need to think about how you'd feel if 32 strangers started petting you. And keep in mind, Koani will be doing many more programs like this. In fact, she's doing another program at your community hall tonight."

Students wait for Koani to arrive.

Through the window, Pat could see Bruce, Koani, and Indy coming toward the door. Pat had one more thing to tell the children, "Please show Koani respect. And remember, she's a teacher, she's not a pet. There's many times when Bruce and I feel sad about having her in captivity. In a perfect world, all wolves would run free in the wild. But in a perfect world, there wouldn't be people who killed wolves because they hated or feared them. Hate and fear usually come from not understanding something. Koani's job is to teach people the truth about wolves and show them that wolves aren't monsters."

The door opened. Indy bounded into the room with his tail wagging and a happy grin on his face. The children giggled and laughed. "Now watch the difference in how Koani enters," said Pat.

A magical hush fell over the children. They stared, wide-eyed, as Koani entered with calm dignity, her yellow eyes blazing with curiosity. With Bruce in tow, Koani circled the room. A boy announced in a frightened voice, "It's a black wolf! They're the most vicious kind!"

"Black, gray, tan and white pups can all be born in the same litter," said Bruce. "Just like in a human family, brothers and sisters can have different-colored hair and eyes. The color of a wolf tells you nothing about its behavior—the same as with people."

Indy (left) comes right into the classroom and makes friends, while Koani stays on her leash.

Students watch as Koani begins to destroy a teddy bear.

At the front of the classroom, Koani followed Indy and jumped on top of a table where everyone could see her better. Pat asked the teacher to come forward. Koani licked the teacher's face and the students laughed. The teacher put a few toys on the table. Koani picked out a plastic doll and chewed on it. She snipped off an arm and next the legs. The children pointed and laughed. "This is another reason that wolves don't make good pets," said Pat. "Wolves would treat your new toys just like bones or an old stick."

Pat and Bruce answered questions and then concluded the program. "For a long time, people in the United States trapped, poisoned, and shot wolves. They wanted to exterminate wolves and they succeeded. For 50 years, we didn't have wolf packs running wild in the Northwest. Now, wolves have traveled down from Canada to live in the Rocky and Cascade Mountains. Whether or not they're successful depends on people's attitudes. The West is settled, the frontier is tamed. Can we allow wolves a place to live, can we tolerate a little wildness? The decision is yours."

They loaded Koani in the van. She paced around inside her kennel and then lay down on the straw. Bruce and Pat sighed with relief and gave each other five. "We did it," said Bruce.

"Koani was great! You know that saying about a picture being worth a thousand words," said Pat. "Well, showing those students Koani was worth a thousand pictures. No television documentary or book could ever be as powerful as the presence of a living animal." All the time they'd spent to prepare Koani for a classroom visit had paid off.

"The day isn't over yet," said Bruce. "There will be a lot of grown-ups who hate wolves at tonight's program."

Koani with Pat and all the students at a one-room school in Idaho

In the Community Hall, Pat and Bruce looked around them. Hecklers rudely interrupted the program. People wearing cowboy hats held protest signs that proclaimed, "The 3 S's: Shoot, Shovel, and Shut Up!" and "No Wolves, No Way!" Their hatred of wolves filled the room with so much tension that the people who liked wolves were scared to admit it.

"Maybe we shouldn't bring Koani in," whispered Pat. "Some of these people are pretty mad about wolves. They might hurt her."

A man wearing a camouflage-colored cap jumped to his feet. "Wolves are nature's criminals!" he screamed.

"She's probably safer in here with us than she is alone in the van," said Bruce and walked out to get her.

Koani, a true teacher

Koani entered the room and all but the most rude people quieted down. They watched her with interest.

The man wearing the camo-colored cap stood up again. He shouted, "Big deal! That animal is tame. A real wolf would've killed somebody by now."

A girl next to the man rose to her feet. One hundred and fifty people quieted as the 12-year-old nervously cleared her throat. "There are adults who will never learn anything." The red-faced man glared at her. She looked straight ahead, "Thank you for coming to the Swan Valley with Koani. We children can learn for ourselves about wolves. We can make up our own minds."

Her courage inspired the people who liked wolves. Applause filled the room. The noise caused Koani to stop chewing on the stuffed toy and stare at the audience. Her eyes looked into the eyes of those who liked wolves and those who did not. Koani had truly become a teacher.

Appendix
Commonly Asked Questions

What can I do to help wolves?

There are two main things you can do to help wolves. You can write to the people who represent you in the federal and state governments. Tell them what you think about wolves.

The most important thing you can do is to learn more about wolves. Talk to friends, relatives, neighbors, and family about wolves and let them know what wolves are really like. Many children think that they're too young for their words to make any difference. That's not true. Remember the story of the brave girl who spoke out in the community hall. She inspired confidence and courage in grown-ups who were frightened to admit that they liked wolves. Her words made a difference. When you learn about things and speak out, you influence the people around you far more than you might think.

If I want a wolf of my own, what should I do?

Wolves don't make good pets. As you can tell from Koani's story, Pat and Bruce spent a lot of time with her every day. Not only that, they founded a nonprofit organization, Wild Sentry, dedicated to environmental education. They spent lots of money to build her enclosure. In addition, Koani isn't a pet, she's a teacher—that's why Bruce and Pat agreed to raise her, so she could teach people about the true nature of her brothers and sisters in the wild.

If you really, really want to be in the company of wolves, there are zoos and wolf sanctuaries, education centers, and research organizations you can work or volunteer for.

When was Koani born?

Koani was born in captivity on May 5, 1991. She's a Cinco de Mayo baby. Unlike dogs, all wolves have their birthdays in April or May. Indy is six months older than Koani.

What kind of wolf is Koani?

Koani is a gray wolf. There are two basic types of wolves, the gray wolf and red wolf. Gray wolves inhabited most of North America from the Pacific to the Atlantic Coast and from Alaska clear down to southern Mexico; they also lived in most of Europe and Asia. Humans have dramatically reduced the range of gray wolves; most of them now live in Alaska, Canada, and Siberia. Red wolves historically lived in the southeastern United States. Most red wolves now live in zoos, except for a few wild ones in North Carolina. In different parts of the country, people call the gray wolf a timber wolf, buffalo wolf, or Arctic wolf.

Do wolf-dog hybrids make good pets?

Wolf-dog hybrids are part wolf and part dog. Most hybrids don't make good pets. A hybrid can have the traits of a dog that make it less fearful of people, mixed with the instinctive predatory traits of the wolf. Such a mix can be a recipe for disaster. Unfortunately, no one can tell until the hybrid is an adult whether it will be dangerous and hard to handle. Most hybrids are dead by the time they're two years old. By that time, the hybrid is likely to have been killed by someone else after it has escaped and caused trouble. If it hasn't been killed, the owner has probably discovered that the animal is not a good pet. The owner may then euthanize the animal or turn it loose in the woods, where it will starve to death because it has never learned to hunt.

Koani and Indy "help" Pat ski.

Is Indy part wolf? What kind of dog is Indy?

No, Indy is not a wolf. He is pure dog. Because he came from the animal shelter, Bruce and Pat don't know exactly what kind of dog he is. They call him a Big Sky Snowroller.

Can Koani have puppies?

Koani has been neutered so that she can't have puppies. There are many people who breed and sell wolves. Unfortunately, most people who get a wolf never stopped to really think about the responsibilities they were taking on. After it's too late, they realize that wolves don't make good pets. There are too

many wolves in captivity, and most of them end up dead before the age of two. Bruce and Pat don't want to contribute to the problem.

Do wolves get married?

Before wolves mate and have babies, they go through a courtship and decide whether or not they like each other. After they have pups, the male and female wolves often stay together until one of them dies. They don't have weddings with fancy clothes, gifts, and a minister like humans do. So you'll have to decide for yourself if wolves are married or not.

Are wild wolves dangerous to people?

There's never been a documented case of a healthy wild wolf killing anyone in North America. This isn't to say that they never have or never will kill a human, but such an occurrence would be very rare. We do have documented cases of deer killing people with their antlers or hooves every year, and yet people aren't scared of deer. You're in far more danger driving down the road in a car than you'd ever be in the woods, no matter what kind of predators lived there.

Koani gets to know some cows (below) and plays with a bone in the pond in her enclosure.

What kind of fence does Koani have?

Two fences surround Koani's enclosure. The outer fence is 8 feet high. Four feet in from it, there's another fence that's 10 feet high. The outer fence stops people from reaching in to Koani's pen. The inner fence keeps Koani in her enclosure. There is also a 4-foot skirt of fencing buried at the base of the inner fence to keep Koani from digging her way out.

Koani feeds on an elk that a mountain lion killed a few hours earlier.

What does Koani eat?

Koani eats 2 to 3 pounds of raw meat every day. The meat is usually deer or elk. Pat and Bruce get scrap meat from the butcher shop during the hunting season. Koani also eats as much as she wants of high-quality dry dog food.

Does Koani hunt?

Being on a 60-foot leash allows Koani to move around a lot. She often catches mice and voles. She has also caught grouse, rabbits, squirrels, and even a muskrat.

Is Koani ever off-leash when she is on a walk?

No, but not because she'd run away. Bruce and Pat are her pack, and even if she got off-leash, Koani would return to them. She is always on a leash or in her pen because wolves can't be trained to obey commands. If Koani ran loose, she might hurt pets or small children.

Could Koani ever be released in the wild?

There are three main reasons why releasing Koani would be irresponsible and cruel. First, Koani is used to being around people and sees them as providers of food. If she were dropped off in the wilderness, she would travel until she found people. People might shoot her out of fear or because Koani chased their pets or livestock. Second, if that didn't happen, she'd starve to death. Wolves learn hunting techniques from their packs. No one has taught Koani how to hunt big animals. Third, Koani could not join another pack. If she met up with a pack, they would chase her away or kill her.

Why wouldn't a pack of wolves adopt Koani?

A pack of wolves is a family; they're all related. Think of your family gathered at the table to eat dinner. If a stranger walked in and started taking things out of the refrigerator, what would your family do?

How do new packs get started?

Some wolves stay with their family all their lives. Other "teenage" (10- to 24-month-old) wolves decide to leave their family and home territory; this is called **dispersal.** Dispersing wolves can travel 500 miles, but usually they travel less than 100 miles. When they find a place that doesn't already have a wolf pack, they stop traveling. There they wait, in hopes of meeting and liking a dispersing wolf from another pack. If they do, they have pups together, and a new pack begins.

When are the pups born?

Wolves mate in late February and give birth to 4 to 6 pups 62 to 63 days later, in April or May. Pups spend the first 2 to 3 weeks with their mother. After that the pups crawl out of the den and the entire pack helps raise them. They begin hunting with the pack when they're around 6 months old.

How fast can wolves run?

For a short sprint, wolves can run 35 to 40 miles per hour. They can trot or lope along at 5 miles per hour for hours on end and can travel 120 miles a day.

How strong are the jaws of a wolf?

Wolves need strong jaws to catch their prey. The jaws of a wolf have a crushing power of 1,500 pounds per square inch, compared to a German Shepherd with 750 pounds per square inch. The jaws of a wolf are stronger than any dog's. Strong jaws also allow wolves to crush bones to get at the nutritious marrow.

How much do wolves weigh?

Most wolves weigh somewhere between 70 and 120 pounds. Males weigh about 10 percent more than females. Sometimes (as with humans) there is an exceptionally large wolf. The largest wolf ever found was from Alaska and weighed 165 pounds. At 100 pounds, Koani is a large female.

Above: *Koani at five months old, at which time she gained half a pound each day.* Right: *Koani explores Anasazi ruins in Utah.*

When are wolves adults?

Wolves reach full size when they are 8 to 10 months old. They usually don't breed until they are at least 22 months old.

How long do wolves live?

Wild wolves usually don't live much longer than eight or nine years. The reason they don't live longer is that by that age they have arthritis from being kicked by prey animals, and their teeth are broken and worn down. When these things happen, they can't get enough to eat and they starve. In captivity, wolves die of old age between the ages of 13 and 17 years.

Do wolves ever eat other wolves?

While it's not uncommon for wolves to kill other wolves from strange packs, they usually don't eat them. However, if they are extremely hungry, they sometimes do. Just like people, wolves have been known to eat their own kind, though it's very rare.

Where do wolves live?

Wolves can live in almost any environment as long as there are plenty of prey animals. They used to live in forests, plains, tundra, and deserts. The only places they didn't do well were high mountains, tropical swampy areas and extreme deserts, probably because there wasn't enough for them to eat in those places.

Wolves used to live all over North America. How come there aren't very many of them in the lower 48 states now?

Wolves all over North America were poisoned and trapped until they were exterminated from most of the lower 48 states by the 1930s. This was done because they killed livestock. One reason they did was that people killed most of the native prey such as the bison and elk, so wolves didn't have anything else to eat. People also killed wolves because they believed the bad stories they'd heard about them.

What do wolves need to survive?

Wolves need two main things to survive. They need to be safe from people killing them. Most important, they need habitat. Habitat is the area that has everything an animal needs to survive. A wolf's habitat must support large numbers of prey animals. If people keep building homes in all the valleys, there won't be places for the prey animals to spend the winter. When prey animals disappear, the wolves won't have anything to eat.

Wild Sentry

The name Wild Sentry means a guardian of wildness. If wolves live in an area, then you know that the land is truly wild, free, and healthy. Wolves are also guardians of the wild herd animals that they hunt. Because wolves prey on sicker, weaker, and older animals, the stronger, quicker, and smarter deer, elk, bison, moose, caribou, and musk ox live to pass their superior traits on to future generations. Wolves also keep prey animals from overpopulating an area, which means that the land is better able to provide enough food for the herd.

Wild Sentry is a nonprofit organization that presents factual, high-quality environmental programs to schools and the general public. By combining science with the humanities, Wild Sentry's programs entertain as well as inform.

There are a few places in the country where wolves are returning to the lands they once lived in before being exterminated. The return of wolves has sparked a very emotional controversy. Few people have seen a wolf; nevertheless they hold strong opinions based on campfire tales, legend, and folklore.

As a teacher and an ambassador for her species, Koani helps people get over their fear of wolves and to learn the truth about an animal that stalks the human imagination. In addition to Koani, the program features Indy, the cutest dog in the world. It also features an entertaining natural history lecture, lively stories, and a fascinating slide show presented by wildlife biologist Pat Tucker and storyteller/writer Bruce Weide.

You can become a member of the Wild Sentry team and receive a photo of Koani and a newsletter that describes the further adventures of Koani, Indy, Pat, and Bruce. For information write to:

Wild Sentry
Box 172
Hamilton, MT 59840

Glossary

alpha: the dominant member (or pair) of a group such as a pack

bond: an attachment that an individual human or animal forms to another. Many animals such as wolves have difficulty forming strong bonds to another individual or species when they are no longer infants.

canine: a member of a family of animals that includes dogs, wolves, foxes, and coyotes

dispersal: the process in which young wolves leave their families to form new packs

domestication: the process by which wild animals become suited to living with humans

dominant: being in charge of, or leading, others. A dominant wolf holds its tail up, pricks its ears, and stands tall around a submissive wolf.

euthanize: to kill as painlessly as possible. When we can't find a home for an animal, or if it is suffering and we can't relieve its pain or cure it, it is euthanized.

exterminate: to deliberately and completely kill all the members of a group or species

instincts: things that an animal is born knowing how to do

pack: a group that gathers together to make hunting and other ways of surviving easier

predators: animals that hunt and kill other animals

regurgitate: to throw up or vomit. When canines regurgitate, it does not necessarily mean that they are sick.

social: preferring the company of other creatures rather than being alone. Animals that are social like to be around each other and usually gather in a group.

submit: to let another animal boss or lead. Submissive wolves lower their tails, lay their ears back, and roll over on their backs around dominant wolves.

territorial: to consider an area of land as your own and to keep strange members of your species out by using warnings or fighting, if needed. Animals such as deer that are not territorial are said to have home ranges. This means that they have certain areas where they live but they don't defend them.

wolfers: men who were hired to kill wolves by people who didn't want any wolves around

Index

19-601